GĪTĀNIDARŚANA

Gītānidarśana

Similes of the Bhagavadgītā

ANANTANAND RAMBACHAN

MOTILAL BANARSIDASS PUBLISHERS
PRIVATE LIMITED ● DELHI

First Edition: Delhi, 1999

ISBN: 81-208-1695-1

Also available at:

MOTILAL BANARSIDASS

236 Sri Ranga, 9th Main III Block, Jayanagar, Bangalore 560 011
41 U.A. Bungalow Road, Jawahar Nagar, Delhi 110 007
8 Mahalaxmi Chamber, Warden Road, Mumbai 400 026
120 Royapettah High Road, Mylapore, Chennai 600 004
Sanas Plaza, 1302, Baji Rao Road, Pune 411 002
8 Camac Street, Calcutta 700 017
Ashok Rajpath, Patna 800 004
Chowk, Varanasi 221 001

PRINTED IN INDIA
BY JAINENDRA PRAKASH JAIN AT SHRI JAINENDRA PRESS,
A-45 NARAINA, PHASE I, NEW DELHI 110 028
AND PUBLISHED BY NARENDRA PRAKASH JAIN FOR
MOTILAL BANARSIDASS PUBLISHERS PRIVATE LIMITED,
BUNGALOW ROAD, DELHI 110 007

for Shashi, Kumud, Prasanna and Usha
our friends
who make Minnesota
a place of warmth

Contents

Preface

The Bhagavadgita (ca.300 BCE), which literally means "the song of God," is a dialogue between the teacher, Krishna and his friend and disciple, Arjuna. This conversation is called "the song of God" because Krishna is revered in the Hindu tradition as an incarnation of God.

The Bhagavadgita consists of seven hundred verses and is to be found in a much larger text called the Mahabharata (400 BCE - 400 CE). The Mahabharata is traditionally attributed to the author, Vyasa, although the name means "compiler." The Mahabharata consists of 100,00 verses and is the longest work in Indian literary history. It is four times the length of the Bible and eight times the length of the Greek epics, the Illiad and Odessy, combined.

The central narrative of the Mahabharata tells the story of the conflict between two set of cousins in North India, the Kauravas and the Pandavas. The Pandavas have been cheated out of their legitimate share of the family kingdom and have suffered many injustices at the hands of the Kauravas. All efforts to settle the matter peacefully failed because of the selfishness and obstinacy of the Kaurava leader Duryodhana. Krishna himself tried unsuccessfully to mediate and made a futile plea for compromise. War was inevitable and Krishna offered to serve as the charioteer of Arjuna.

On the day of the battle, Arjuna requested Krishna to drive his chariot between the two armies in order to survey the opposing forces. When he looked at the soldiers arrayed against him, he was shocked to recognize many friends, family members and teachers. Although they were prepared to wage an unjust war, Arjuna felt that he could not engage in battle against those with whom he had such close relationships. He was prepared to concede victory to the Kauravas.

Arjuna turned to his friend, Krishna, and asked his guidance. "My mind is confused," said Arjuna,"as to my duty. I ask you to tell me clearly what is best for me. I am your disciple, please instruct me." Krishna complied and a conversation of deep philosophical and practical significance developed. While Krishna's immediate purpose in the Bhagavadgita was to persuade Arjuna to fulfill his obligations to his community by defending it against tyranny and injustice, Arjuna asked many questions about the goal of human existence, the causes of evil, and the nature of right action. Krishna answered him in detail and, in several of his answers, offered a dynamic reinterpretation of traditional teachings.

The Bhagavadgita, as mentioned above, is a dialogue between Krishna, the teacher, and Arjuna, his disciple. The essential subject-matter of the discussion is the nature of the absolute (*brahman*) which is not different from the human self (*ātman*). The purpose of the discussion is to help Arjuna understand the nature of the self so that he may act on the basis of this wisdom. Arjuna has to discover himself and grasp the logic of Krishna's arguments.

Since understanding, and not mere belief, is the aim of Krishna's methods, he employs various teaching strategies to aid Arjuna's comprehension and to remove his doubts and misunderstandings. He often explains a difficult statement with the aid of a simile drawn from everyday human experience and the Bhagavadgita contains some of the most suggestive and beautiful similes in the entire sacred literature of Hinduism. Krishna uses similes to explain and illustrate abstract arguments, in order to convince Arjuna of the truth of his teachings and to make these accessible to his confused student. The similes of

Krishna add a beautiful visual dimension to words and invite reflection and exploration.

In this text, I have chosen twelve of my favorite similes from the Bhagavadgita for reflection. They deal with diverse but interrelated matters such as the nature of the self, death, scriptures, self-control, peace, wisdom, and the nature of God. They offer an exciting entrance into the Hindu world-view. Each simile presents an inexhaustible richness of meaning and my commentary on each one, therefore, cannot be exhaustive. If the meanings which I draw from these similes awaken you to their beauty and guide you to finding insights of your own, my intention will be fulfilled.

The material contained in this book was presented first as a series of lectures at the Hindu Society of Minnesota during the year 1998. I am grateful to Professor Prasanna Kumar for urging me to make these widely available in book form and to all those who attended my lectures and shared in the discussion. For her unfailing encouragement and helpful suggestions, I am thankful to my wife, Geeta. My friend, Craig Rice, generously gave his time to help with formatting tasks, and my publishers, Motilal Banarsidass, readily consented to this project and its speedy publication.

Chapter 1

The Immortality of the Self

Just as the embodied self enters into childhood, youth and old age, so also does it enter into another body. The wise person is not confused about this. (2:13)[1]

In the twelfth verse of chapter two, Krishna introduced Arjuna to the idea of the immortality of the self (*ātman*). "There was never a time," says Krishna, "when I did not

---

[1] *dehino 'smin yathā dehe*
kaumāraṁ yāuvanaṁ jarā
tathā dehāntaraprāptir
dhīras tatra na muhyati

exist, nor you, nor these leaders. We shall not cease to exist in the future."

Arjuna was confused by Krishna's claim that the self has always and will always exist. As far as Arjuna was concerned, he was born, had gone through the stages of childhood and youth and was rapidly aging. He was a child, a young man and now an adult. Soon, he would grow old and die. How could Krishna claim that he always existed and would exist forever? He may have turned to Krishna, as a student turns to a teacher when a new idea is perplexing, with a look of bewilderment and disbelief.

As a skillful and concerned teacher, Krishna would be trying to ascertain Arjuna's understanding from his facial expressions. Seeing the look of disbelief on Arjuna's face, Krishna offered a brilliant and insightful analogy to help him understand the eternal nature of the self. The beauty of Krishna's example is that it gave Arjuna an opportunity to reflect on the meaning of his own human experience of growth. While this experience is common to us all, Krishna invites us to consider its meaning and what it teaches us about ourselves.

All of us reading these words can recollect some incidents from our childhood. We may remember sitting in an elementary school class or playing with friends at recess. To have a recollection of our elementary school experiences implies that we were present in our childhood bodies when these experiences took place.

Our childhood bodies change and we enter into youthful bodies. Once again, each one of us can recollect some experiences from our youth. We may recollect a party with friends at high school or college. The same truth holds here, and memories from our youth require our presence in our youthful bodies. Youth soon gives way to adulthood and adulthood to old age.

In the movement from childhood to youth, adulthood, and old age, our physical bodies undergo significant change. Our experiences in these stages also differ and, because of these, our memories are correspondingly different. Is there anything constant and unchanging?

The unchanging factor in all four stages, according to the Bhagavadgita, is you or me, the self. The childhood body gave way to a youthful one, the youthful body to a adult body and the adult body to an aged one. When childhood passed away, you did not. With memories of childhood, you lived in your youthful body, and, when this body passed away, you moved with your memories into adult and aged bodies. In a similar way, suggests Krishna, one moves from an aged body, after death, into a new physical body. Our bodies and minds are in a process of continuous change, but the self remains unchanged.

In this simile, the self is referred to as the "dweller in the body (*dehin*)." This term suggests that while we live or dwell in our bodies, we are not the same as our bodies. The changes which the body undergoes in childhood, youth, adulthood and old age do not affect the essential nature of the one who dwells in the body and who is essentially different from it.

If the expression "dweller in the body" makes you think of the body as a house and the self as the one dwelling in it, your image is quite appropriate. Later in the text, Krishna speaks of the body as a city of nine gates and the self as existing within it. Many of us change homes from time to time because of our professions or family commitments. If we are the same as our homes, such changes would not be possible and we would not be able to leave one home and enter into another. In a similar way, while we live in our bodies, we are not identical with our bodies and we continue to be the same when our bodies change. Upon death, we move into a new body as we move into a new dwelling place.

The purpose of Krishna's example is to help us understand that we are not the same as our bodies and that the death of the body is not the death of the self. This knowledge helps to liberate us from the great fear of death. Our fear of death is, in part, a fear of the unknown. Krishna helps us to think of death as a natural stage in the process of life which begins in childhood and progresses through youth, adulthood and old age. Even as childhood "dies" to enable youth to come into being, and youth "dies" to allow the adult to come into being, the death of the body is not the end of existence, but the passage into new life. Death does not signify non-existence, but the continuity of life in a new body. You, the self, was, is and will forever be.

Chapter 2

Death: A Change of Body

Just as a person changes worn-out clothing and
wears new ones, so also does the embodied self
leaves worn-out bodies and enters into other
new ones.(2:22)[2]

The purpose of the previous simile (2:13)
was to help Arjuna understand the eternal nature
of the self. In the movement from childhood,
youth, adulthood and old age, our bodies
undergo change. The self is the common and
constant factor in all stages. It is aware of all

---

[2] vāsāṁsi jīrṇāni yathā vihāya
navāni gṛhṇāti naro 'parāṇi
tathā śarīrāṇi vihāya jīrṇāny
anyāni saṁyāti navāni dehī

bodily and mental changes occurring. Just as it moves from one physical stage to another, so also does it move, at the time of death, into a new body.

In this simile, which is perhaps the most famous one in the entire text, if not in all the Hindu scriptures, Krishna explains the process of moving from one body into another. He again uses a familiar experience to convey an unfamiliar teaching and helps us to overcome fear and anxiety about death by relating it to a common experience.

The obvious point of this striking example is the analogy between the physical body and a suit of clothes. The wearer of clothing is different from the clothing which he or she wears. The clothing is used for various purposes, but is not identical with the wearer. The body is like a suit of clothing in the sense that the one who dwells in the body is different from the body. Like a suit of clothing, one is aware of one's body. One sees it and often speaks of it as an object of possession by referring to it as "my body." Even as the owner of clothing is different from the clothing, the owner of the body is different from the body.

Another insight of this simile is derived from the fact that a change of clothing is an experience of discontinuity and continuity. Discarding clothing is not the same as discarding oneself. Clothing may be changed or disposed, but the wearer continues to be. Similarly, death does not mean the end or extinction of the one who dwells in the body. As the wearer puts on a new suit of clothing, the dweller in the body acquires a new body. In this new body, the original dweller continues to live on.

The Sanskrit term, *jīrṇāni*, which is used twice in this verse to refer both to clothing and bodies means old, but also worn out. While we often discard clothing after these have grown old and tattered, we sometimes use a suit of clothing for a very limited purpose. We may use it for a special occasion such as a wedding or an interview and never use it again. This suit, although used once or twice, is also worn out. It has served its purpose. With reference to clothing, "worn out" is not synonymous with "old."

The same holds true for the change of bodies. Death, as we know too well, does not come only to the aged. The young also die. In the Hindu understanding, the human birth and the body which one inherits are the consequence of actions in previous births, referred to as *karma*. The body is the instrument for potentially pleasurable and painful experiences

as determined by our actions in the past. It is also
the instrument for the initiation and performance
of new actions in the present. Once these
experiences have been gained, the body has
served its purpose and the journey of life
continues in a new body.

We may select one suit of clothing over
another for reasons of appropriateness and
purpose. Our work may require us to wear a
formal suit, but this will not be suitable for a visit
to the gym. The purpose which we have in mind
determines our choice of clothing. Similarly, the
new body which we acquire after the death of
this one is purposeful. While it is true that the
body is a result of past actions, we must
remember that the cycle of birth, death and
rebirth is meant for spiritual growth and
development. It is a process of learning and
each new birth offers the necessary
circumstances for such growth to occur.

The lessons to be learnt will differ for
each one of us. These may be lessons about
compassion, patience, self-control, detachment,
humility and generosity. If we search and
scrutinize our experiences and circumstances, we
will discover the lessons which we need to learn
and how our lives offer opportunities for
learning. There is a relationship between what
we need to learn and the circumstances of our

new lives. Once the appropriate lessons are learnt, new lessons may require new circumstances. The Hindu teaching about *karma* is not primarily about punishment, but about moral and spiritual growth. Even when our actions generate painful consequences, the more profound purpose is to help us appreciate a value or truth which will help us to avoid causing pain to others and to ourselves.

Death, in the Hindu tradition, is generally understood to occur when the results of past actions which have brought the body into existence are exhausted. The important point is that this does not always occur when the body is aged. It is the exhaustion of *karma* and not age which determines the event of death. Krishna uses the plural in this verse and speaks of changing bodies. The reason is that we may have changed many bodies in the past and we may continue to do so in the future until we overcome ignorance and attain God. This attainment brings to an end the cycle of birth, death and rebirth.

While Krishna's simile likens the body to a suit of clothing, we must keep the limited purpose of the example in mind. We would be drawing the wrong conclusion from his example, if we understood the body to be unimportant and lacking in value. Birth as a human being is

consistently praised in the scriptures of Hinduism
and by its great teachers.

The human body is prized because of its
capacity for reason and knowledge. It is a ladder
which enables one to ascend towards God.
Krishna later condemns all actions, including
those performed in the name of religion, which
are detrimental to the well-being of the body.

In comparing the body to a suit of clothing,
however, Krishna reminds us that we are much
more than our bodies. The clothes which we
wear have a limited purpose and we should not
become obsessive about these. Similarly, the
body is a marvelous instrument, but only a finite
one. It is a means and not the end. If it becomes
the center of our lives and attention, we
degenerate into body worship and idolatry.
Hinduism asks us to avoid the harmful extremes
of bodily neglect and bodily worship. This is
what is meant by detachment.

Chapter 3

The Value of Scriptures

For a wise person who knows, all the Vedas have
no more value than a well when there is
water flowing everywhere. (2:46)[3]

    Scriptures, written or oral, are important
sources of authority in the religions of the world.
Judaism, Christianity, Islam and Hinduism are
examples of traditions with written texts, while
many African and Native American traditions
still preserve their sacred teachings orally. While
Hindu texts are available in written form, they
were preserved and transmitted orally for

---

3 *yāvān artha udapāne*
sarvataḥ samplutodake
tāvān sarveṣu vedeṣu
brāhmaṇasya vijānataḥ

centuries and it is still more common for these to be heard than read.

In this verse, we have an important comment by Krishna on the significance and purpose of the scriptures of Hinduism and, in particular, on the Vedas, which are its most authoritative texts. Let us look closely at the example which he uses. In dry seasons, many rivers cease to flow and their sandy beds become visible. Water may be found in these beds, but one would have to dig or drill a hole deep into the bed of the river. It will, of course, be unnecessary to try to dig a hole if the river is flowing with water. Such an effort will be entirely redundant. In a similar way, says Krishna, the Vedas, which are compared here to the well in the bed of a river, become redundant for a person who knows the truth.

The significance of Krishna's example will be appreciated better if we examine the verses immediately preceding this one. In these verses (42-45), Krishna criticizes the unwise persons who are addicted to transient worldly pleasures and power. Such persons do not understand that these goals are ultimately unsatisfactory and cause discontent. These people are not necessarily hostile to religion. They may, on the contrary, be very active religiously. Religion, however, is just a means to attain their desires for pleasure and power. After death, they hope to attain a heavenly world where they expect to enjoy pleasure and power similar to that which they longed for on earth.

What interests such persons are the various religious rituals and ceremonies which promise pleasure and power here and in the hereafter. This is the sum total of their understanding of religion and to these they are intensely devoted. God has no other value than as a means to the fulfillment of personal desires. Their understanding of the scripture is superficial and literal and, even though they may cite it often, they grasp the letter and not the spirit.

The philosophy of life which holds power and pleasure to be the highest goals of human existence here and in the hereafter is an attractive one and its practitioners lure others by engaging in what Krishna describes as flowery speech. A flower is an attractive object, but its beauty is not eternal. Some flowers bloom and preserve their freshness for a day; others may last for as long as a week. Each one eventually fades and withers. Flowery speech paints a rosy and favorable picture of certain goals and ends, like worldly pleasure and power, but ignores their limits and defects.

Hinduism recognizes the legitimate place of pleasure and power in human life. There are various rituals in the first section of the Vedas for the attainment of these. Hinduism, however, does not identify these as the highest goals of human existence.

We live in a world where instant pleasure is encouraged and where flowery speech is used extensively to allure us to indulge ourselves. While pleasure-filled activities, done in moderation, can relieve stress and bring people together, they cannot satisfy the deepest human longings and keep us wanting more and more. Short-lived pleasures cannot provide a secure basis for a meaningful life. The obsession with pleasure and power leaves one discontented, anxious and lonely.

If these goals are intrinsically unsatisfactory on earth, they will also be so in any heavenly world. In addition, the heavenly world is not a permanent one. While it is attained by the performance of meritorious ritual and ethical actions, the fruits of these actions are non-eternal and, upon their exhaustion, one returns to the world of mortality.

The Hindu teaching, however, does not condemn us to rushing madly from one form of limited pleasure to another. While it does not deter us from enjoying pleasures in moderation and faithfulness to basic moral values, its true purpose is to lead us to an understanding of our true self, where we are united with God and where there is lasting joy and peace which we seek. It is in this timeless self that true security and contentment are to be found. When we discover and own it and our lives become filled with enduring peace, we feel no need to rush thoughtlessly after transient forms of enjoyment. One does not reject these, but one is not also stubbornly attached to them. In relation to joy and peace of the self, they become like wells in the bed of a flowing river.

We can understand Krishna's example not just as a comment on the limitations of pleasure and power and on religious rituals which are centered on these, but also as an important reminder about the nature and purpose of the scriptures.

Our scriptures are not just to be ceremoniously read and honored as religious icons. They impart a religious wisdom which challenges us to look at ourselves and to develop a new understanding of ourselves. They offer a perspective which must be understood and internalized by us and brought to bear in our daily lives. When the wisdom of the scripture becomes alive in us and is the nourishing water of our daily life, then the text, oral or written, becomes like a well in a bed of flowing water.

Krishna's simile reminds us that we often run the risk of venerating the physical text and worshipping its words without incorporating these and bringing them to life in our lives. Even as a parents fulfills his or her role when the child grows up into a responsible and independent adult who is no longer dependent on the parents, the scripture fulfills itself when its wisdom is integrated and expressed in our lives. Words must become alive in thought and action.

We must be careful, however, that we do not, because of arrogance or self-deception, think that we have no need for the wisdom or guidance of the scripture. In the example of Krishna, the water in the well becomes unnecessary only when the river is flooded - not before. The scripture becomes redundant only when its teachings have been assimilated into our lives. In times of drought, one will have to return to the well in the river-bed for water. Similarly, even a wise person may have to return to the scripture, from time to time, for inspiration and guidance.

Water in a well is useful, but it is unmoving. It does not flow. The water of a river, however, is dynamic and adapts itself to its environment as it travels towards the ocean. There is something instructive in the contrast between the water of a well and that of a river, even though the essence of water is the same in both. Scriptures undoubtedly contain timeless and eternal wisdom, but they also belong to particular historical periods and cultures and reflect the characteristics of their own epochs. All great scriptures contain teachings which are normative and contextual. The normative teachings are universally valid, but the contextual ones belong to a specific time period and society.

In reading our scriptures, we must be attentive to this fact. If a religion makes its contextual teachings normative, it may soon become irrelevant. Normative teachings define the uniqueness of any religion, but these must have the vigor, freshness and adaptability of a river in flow. They must be enlivened by human experience and speak to contemporary issues and challenges. A scripture which lacks the dynamism of flowing water will soon grow stagnant and cease to be of service to its people.

Chapter 4

Vigilance and Control

When the mind succumbs to the wandering senses, it steals one's wisdom, just as the wind carries away a ship on the waters. (2:67)[4]

In this simile, Krishna uses the example of a ship on the ocean to teach about the nature and importance of self-control. Self-control is an issue for human beings since we possess the ability to exercise choice over our actions. One cannot admonish or instruct one's pet to exercise

---

[4] *indriyāṇāṁ hi caratāṁ*
yan mano 'nuvidhīyate
tadasya harati prajñāṁ
vāyur nāvam ivāmbhasi

self-control since it does not have the ability to choose. Its behavior is regulated by biological drives. Self-control presupposes the exercise of free-will and the ability to decide between alternative courses of action.

The boat in Krishna's example is a sailboat. The Bhagavadgita as a written text is generally thought to date from the second or third century and this is the type of boat with which he would have been familiar. A boatman sails his boat with a particular destination in mind. If the boat is caught in a sudden and strong wind, it may be swept off its course and tossed around helplessly. It could drift aimlessly from its destination and, in the worst case scenario, overturn and be destroyed.

The likelihood of a boat being swept off its course by a strong wind increases if the sailor is inattentive to changes in his environment or if he lacks the necessary skill to control the boat in unfavorable water. A skillful sailor may be able to adjust his sails to make an even violent wind favorable and to use it to reach his destination.

How does this example apply to our human situation? The ocean represents the world and it is common in Hinduism to speak of the world as an ocean and of life as a journey across it. The destination of the boat is the shore where lies the sailor's home and where there is peace, happiness and freedom from fear and danger. The shore is liberation (*mokṣa*), the attainment of God in whom there is no sorrow. The wind represents the mind which is led by the senses, while the boat stands for wisdom or understanding. When the mind comes under the control of the unruly senses, one's wisdom is lost.

Hinduism does not condemn the senses or the enjoyment of sense objects. It does not encourage hate and revulsion for our bodies or the world. Krishna (2:64) praises a person who is able to enjoy the objects of the senses and who neither hates nor is obsessed with these. Such a person enjoys peace.

At the same time, we must be aware that the senses are extroverted and oriented towards the external world. If the senses were not turned outwards, they would not serve us as instruments of knowledge. They must be capable of grasping their respective objects.

Let us think for a moment about the act of eating which is connected particularly with the sense of taste. It is quite possible that we could have had the physical need for food without the accompanying sense of taste. Eating would not be a pleasurable experience and we would be deprived of the data which the sense of taste gives to help us distinguish between desirable and undesirable foods.

The creation is full of wonderfully tasting foods and it is surely the intention of the creator that we enjoy these. The sense of taste affords pleasure and helps to maintain our health. For any number of reasons, it is possible for the desire for food to get out of control with disastrous physical and mental consequences. Such an addiction may become a powerful force, like a storm on the ocean, resistant to the appeals of wisdom and reason. Addiction is self-defeating because, by destroying health, it also reduces the pleasure of eating.

What is true of the sense of taste is also true of any one of the senses. Any sense which grows out of control may bring about ruin and self-destruction.

While the senses are extrovert and oriented to the world, they need the mind for their proper functioning. They are unable to operate independently of the mind. The problem, according to Krishna, is when the mind falls under the sway of the unruly senses. The senses take control of the mind and drag it along the path of addiction and sorrow.

Although this is possible and happens frequently, it is the dependence of the senses on the mind which gives us the ability to exercise freedom and self-control. Self-control would be impossible if the senses functioned independently of the mind. The senses are powerful, but more powerful than the senses is the mind, and more powerful than the mind is wisdom and reason.

When the mind is illumined by wisdom, it is able to assume control of the senses and steer the human being to the safe shore of peace and happiness. The mind becomes a leader and not a follower of the senses. Wisdom is an appreciation of the fact that intemperance and indulgence do not lead to happiness.

Wisdom requires vigilance and alertness. Krishna speaks about the loss of wisdom when the mind is carried along the senses. One must assume, therefore, that he is speaking about a person who possesses wisdom. How could there be a loss of self-control in the presence of wisdom? The problem may be one where the force of established habits reasserts itself through inattentiveness or unmindfulness. These are the times when we speak and act before careful thought about consequences. The scripture obviously accepts this possibility and wants to remind us that the price of self-control and freedom is vigilance. Like a skillful sailor, a

wise person, mindful of the world and his
reactions to it, cán control and check negative
responses before being overwhelmed. Such a
person, like a good sailor, reaches the shore of
peace.

Chapter 5

The Attainment of Peace

A person into whom all desires enter as waters enter the ocean, which, though filled from all sides remains unmoved, attains peace, not the one who lusts after objects of desire. (2:70)[5]

In this serene simile, Krishna uses the example of the ocean to teach about peace and its attainment. The waters of numerous rivers flow into the ocean, which remains still and unmoved. Similarly, a person who encounters the

---

5 *āpūryamāṇam acalapratiṣṭham*
samudram āpaḥ praviśanti yadvat
tadvat kāmā yam praviśanti sarve
sa śāntim āpnoti na kāmakāmī

world, as the ocean receives the rivers flowing
into it, attains peace. Peace is not for the one
who is always desiring things.

Why does the one who lusts after objects
of desire not attain peace? Krishna is speaking
here about greed, and, while greed comes in
many forms, such as the greed for power, control
and fame, he appears to have in mind greed for
material things. Wealth, in Hinduism, is a
legitimate goal of human existence and never
condemned. Greed is the immoderate and
uncontrolled desire for wealth. Greed is
insatiable and cannot coexist with peace.

Human beings seek wealth for a variety of
purposes. It is often a means for the satisfaction
of pleasure through the acquisition   and
enjoyment of homes, cars, food, vacations, and
clothing. The goals of wealth may be more
intangible ones such as social prestige, esteem,
power and control over other human beings. For
some, the acquisition of wealth offers a thrill of
its own, not unlike that of a fisherman who finds
delight in the catch, but not because of real need.

Any one of these motives, pleasure,
prestige, power, or thrill may easily grow out of
control and lure us into an insatiable greed.
Greed is incompatible with peace because it is a
condition of discontent which keeps one feeling

that one never has enough. This is especially so when the goals for which one seeks wealth are exclusive in nature. An exclusive goal gains its value and meaning from the fact that it is not evenly distributed. Social prestige, for example, is not shared equally by all and gains significance from this fact. One must always be ahead of others. If it becomes the central goal in one's life and if one's wealth is a means to it, one will never be contented. One is constantly evaluating one's prestige in relation to others, feeling threatened by the accomplishment of others and lusting for more. How much social recognition does one need to be contented with oneself?

Even legitimate reasons for seeking wealth can become obsessive and out of control. One of the reasons why most people seek wealth is to ensure security in old age, in times of illness or in case of disability. It is wise to plan for such possibilities, but wrong to allow oneself to be so tormented by fears and thoughts about the future that one falls into the river of greed and fails to live life fully in the present. Obsession about the future may also cause miserliness.

The negative effects of greed are not limited to the loss of individual peace. When our lives are dominated by the greed for wealth, our values become distorted and human relationships become superficial. The traditional distinction between instrumental and intrinsic values is helpful for illustrating this point. An object which has instrumental value is desired not for itself but because it enables us to gain something else. A car, for example, has instrumental value as a means of transportation. Something of intrinsic value, on the other hand, is desired and cherished for its own sake. We love our spouses because love is meaningful in itself. [6]

When we are driven by the greed for wealth, we lose sight of this distinction and intrinsic values become instrumental ones. We cultivate friendships, not for the delights of human relationships, but because a particular person may be of economic value to us. We seek a partner in marriage, not for love, but because of his or her economic worth. Even God becomes of instrumental value when we seek God only with particular material motives in mind.

Greed debases and reduces human relationships to an economic value. One's own worth is also determined by one's economic assets. "What is he worth?" is a question that particularly expresses our modern outlook. The question is not "What is the worth of his

---

[6]For a good discussion on this distinction see Solomon Schimmel, *The Seven Deadly Sins* (New York: Oxford University Press, 1997), p. 174.

possessions?" but "What is he worth?" The answer is also expressed in an economic quantity which equates the value of the human being with the value of possessions. Wealth, as we know too well, does not have a fixed value. It varies with complex market factors and when human worth is reduced to an economic factor, the value of a person and his self-esteem become variable. What is the worth of a human being, if such a question could not be answered in economic terms?

At the end of the third chapter of the Bhagavadgita, Arjuna asks an important and interesting question to Krishna. "What is it which drives a person, even unwillingly, to commit evil, as if urged by force?" "It is greed," answers Krishna. In this reply, Krishna points to the fact that greed has social consequences and not merely individual ones. The Mahabharata war, which forms the setting for the dialogue between Krishna and Arjuna, was caused by the greed of Duryodhana for power and wealth. In the Ramayana, Ravana's desire for Sita deafened him to all pleas for peace and led to his downfall. The Savings and Loans scandal of the 1980's in the United States was fueled by greed and information coming out of the tobacco trials underlines the tragic consequences of placing profits ahead of human welfare.

A greedy person encounters and interacts
with the world on the basis of his unquenchable
desires. He is like a voracious fire, destructive
and discontented. The contrast is the ocean which
accommodates rivers without being disturbed.
The stillness of the ocean is like the fullness of a
person who has discovered the intrinsic worth of
the self, which is free from birth and death, and
which is peace. This liberates from greed and
enables one to encounter the world from a deep
inner peace, not easily shaken. The self-worth of
such a person is rooted in his or her own nature
and not dependent on the variable value of
possessions. Even when there is intense activity
on the surface, there is stillness within, as in the
depths of the ocean.

Chapter 6

The Loss of Wisdom

As fire is obscured by smoke, as a mirror by dust, as an embryo is enveloped by the amnion, so too is wisdom covered by greed (3:38)[7]

In chapter three (36-37), Arjuna asks Krishna to identify the motive which drives human beings to do evil. "It is greed," answers Krishna, "it is anger....all-consuming and most sinful. Know this to be the enemy here." Krishna followed this statement with a simile in which he

---

[7] *dhūmenāvriyate vahnir*
yathā 'darśo malena ca
yatholbenāvṛto garbhas
tathā tenedam āvṛtam

used three examples to explain the way in which greed and anger obscure wisdom:

> as a fire is obscured by smoke
> as a mirror by dust
> as an embryo is enveloped by the amnion

In all three examples, wisdom is identified with the flame, mirror and embryo, while greed and anger are likened to smoke, dust and the amnion. Smoke, dust and the amnion conceal the true nature of their respective objects. The brilliance of the flame, the luster of the mirror and the form of the embryo are all concealed. In a similar way, a mind which is enveloped by greed and anger gets a false picture of reality, which is seen only through the lens of its passion.

Why does Krishna use three similes in this verse to illustrate the concealment of wisdom? Each one represents desires of different quality and intensity and varying degrees of anger. When a flame is concealed by smoke, a gentle wind is all that is necessary to blow the smoke away and reveal the flame. Similarly, the mind of a person who is good and wise could be possessed by a desire which may momentarily obscure his or her understanding. Such a person is usually able to control a desire before the mind is obsessed by it. In the terminology of the

Bhagavadgita, this type of person is pure (*sāttvic*).

In the case of a mirror obscured by dust, greater effort is needed to clean and polish the mirror in order to restore its luster. These are desires of a stronger intensity, the non-fulfillment of which cause us to become angry and bitter. Such desires may characterize the personality type described in the Bhagavadgita as passionate (*rājasic*), and includes the longing for power, fame and wealth. Because of the nature of the personality and the intensity of the desires, these are much more difficult to overcome and greater effort is necessary.

In the case of the embryo in the womb, there is almost complete concealment. The embryo emerges only after a slow process of growth and maturation. Growth cannot be hastened by untimely outward intervention. The personality here is characterized by inertia (*tāmasic*). Such a person has a materialistic outlook on life and wisdom is obscured by the desires of the body. Evolution and growth through time is needed for spiritual awakening and the development of wisdom.

It is significant to note that Krishna (3:37) speaks of greed as the cause of sin but does not specify a particular greed. We should conclude from this that greed comes in many forms and guises, including the greed for material objects, status, prestige and power. Greed in any one of these forms obscures wisdom and drives us to commit evil.

The Bhagavadgita (3:40) describes greed as an insatiable fire. Like a raging fire, consuming everything in its path, a person who is consumed by greed tramples over everyone who is perceived as an obstacle to the attainment of his desire. He is in a mad rush towards the object of his desire and heedless of those who are destroyed in the process.

Throughout the text, Krishna makes the connection between greed and anger. In 5:27, he mentions that a happy person is one who is able, on earth, to resist the impulses of greed and anger. In 16:21, greed and anger constitute the gate leading to suffering. Anger is aroused by the frustration of greed and is an important emotion at work in crimes of various kinds. Together with greed, it impedes and obscures wisdom.

In chapter two (62-63), Krishna gives an insightful sequence of the steps through which an individual personality disintegrates.

When a person dwells on the objects
of the senses, attachment to them is
born. From attachment arises greed,
and from greed, anger is born.

From anger comes confusion, and
from confusion, the loss of memory.
From the loss of memory comes the
destruction of reason, and from the
destruction of reason, one perishes.

By continuously thinking of an object one
grows attached to it. Attachment leads to greed
and unfulfilled greed to anger. Anger stirs up a
cloud of confusion which settles over the mind
and hampers one's ability to properly assess and
respond to any situation. In a reflective moment,
we are surprised and full of regret about our
words and actions in a state of anger. We admit
that we lose control of ourselves. A person who is
not normally violent or abusive may be so in a fit
of anger.

Under the angry clouds of confusion, one's
memory is impaired. Long-standing relationships
are forgotten. We always magnify the faults of
those with whom we are angry. While a single
act or word may have offended us, the person
stands condemned totally. The next step is the
loss of reason which comes as a consequence of

the loss of memory and the disregarding of relationships and norms of behavior. An angry person is usually impermeable to appeals of reason. If one does not recover one's reason, one's actions may be destructive of others and of oneself.

Understanding the connection between greed and anger is an important step in overcoming both. As long as our lives are dominated by greed of one kind or another, the likelihood of being caught in the grip of anger is high. Greed is overcome when one discovers a fullness in life which makes greed redundant. This fullness is one's own true nature, found in the depths of oneself where one is united with God.

Chapter 7

Offering Actions to God

One who works, giving up attachment, and offering all actions to the infinite, is not stained by sin, like a lotus leaf is not stained by water.

(5:10)[8]

The image of a lotus leaf unstained by water is a popular one in Hinduism. The lotus plant grows in a lake or pond, surrounded by water on all sides. The leaf of the lotus, however, is never wet or waterlogged. If water

---

[8] *brahmaṇy ādhāya karmāṇi*
saṅgaṁ tyaktvā karoti yaḥ
lipyate na sa pāpena
padmapattram ivāmbhasā

is poured on a lotus leaf, it simply rolls off, leaving the leaf dry. The lotus leaf, living in the midst of water and uncontaminated by it, is a powerful symbol of purity and faithfulness. In a similar way, suggests Krishna, a person who offers all his actions to God is uncontaminated by sin.

What does it mean to offer one's actions to God? To offer one's actions to God is to do these with the attitude that one is serving God. Actions are offered to God when they become an expression of one's love for God. Daily actions are performed with the consciousness that one is serving and worshipping God. This differentiates an act of worship from an ordinary action.

An action which is outwardly religious, like visiting a temple or worshipping in one's home, is not truly religious unless it is done for God.   An act, on the other hand, which is not usually thought of as religious, like teaching in a classroom or coaching soccer, becomes religious if done with the attitude of serving God.

Sri Ramakrishna told the story of two friends who were going for a walk when they passed the doorway of a temple where the scriptures were being read and discussed. One friend entered the temple and asked the other to join him. His friend took a peep and continued

further down the street where there was a
popular casino. After entering the casino and
gambling for a while, he felt disgusted with
himself. "Shame on me," he thought. "My friend
is listening to the sacred text and I am wasting
my time and losing my money." His friend, in
the temple, was imagining the pleasures of the
casino and wishing that he had chosen to go
there. In the course of time, both friends died.
The messenger of death came for the soul of the
man who had gone to the temple. While his body
was in the temple, his heart was in the casino.
The messenger of God came for the soul of the
one who had gone to the casino. While his body
was in the casino, his heart was in the temple.
The point of the story is not that the casino is
preferable to the temple but that, in worship, one
must be present in mind and heart.

If offering our actions to God means doing
everything as a way of serving and expressing
love for God, we must recognize that this is not
the same as performing actions for a human
being. God is the creator of the universe, its
supporter and the source and origin of all its
laws. To perform action for God is to recognize
that the outcome of these actions is ultimately
dependent on God's will. We choose our goals
and work energetically for their accomplishment.
We understand that we do not have complete
control over the outcome. God is the giver of the

results of actions. We may choose the actions which we do, but the results of these are not fully within our control.

What are the mental and emotional effects of performing our actions and entrusting the results to God? One of the significant causes of anxieties in our daily life is worry about the outcomes of our actions. These anxieties can intensify and cripple our ability to act effectively. When the results of our actions are entrusted to God, we free ourselves from the burden of worry and are able to apply ourselves more efficiently to the tasks before us. The quality of our actions improve when our minds are absorbed in the means and not fixated on the end.

One of my teachers loved to tell the story of a vendor who took a basket of vegetables each morning for sale at the local market.[9] He stood at the roadside awaiting the arrival of the bus which transported him to the market. When the bus arrived, he would look for an empty seat, but always kept the basket on his head. Even when an empty seat was available next to him or there was space on the floor, he kept the basket on his head. One day, a curious passenger inquired about this unusual habit. "The bus,"

---

9 Swami Dayananda Saraswati

replied the vendor, "carries the weight of all these passengers. I have no desire to add to its burden by putting my basket of vegetables down!"

The vendor did not understand that the bus was already carrying the weight of his basket. Similarly, when we surrender the outcome of our actions to God, we must entrust our anxieties as well. We should not be weighed down by anxieties about the outcome, even as the lotus leaf is not weighed down by water.

Our anxieties about work are not only connected with fears about the outcome. We suffer also when the outcome is realized, and it is not the one which we expect. If we entrust the outcome to God, however, we must be prepared to accept this outcome, favorable and unfavorable, as coming from God. The difficulty is that we are usually willing to accept desirable outcomes as coming from God, but not the undesirable ones. A devotee learns to see the hand of God in both kinds of results and maintains an equilibrium. She is happy in a desirable outcome, although her rejoicing is not an egotistic exhilaration. At the same time, an undesirable outcome does not plunge her into the depths of depression and cripple her ability to act. If an undesirable outcome does not have the power to unbalance us mentally and emotionally,

we have achieved equilibrium and detachment.
This is the attitude to action recommended by
Krishna (2:48).

> Fixed in Yoga, Arjuna, do your
> work, giving up attachment and
> remaining peaceful in both success
> and failure. This equilibrium of
> mind is called Yoga.

Peace of mind, when the outcome of an action is
realized, is a state of purity, comparable to that
of a lotus leaf in water. The mind is neither
burdened by success nor failure.

This does not mean that one is unable to
differentiate a desirable outcome from an
undesirable one. It means composure in success
and failure. If the sense of failure "sticks" to us
and becomes a burden, like water on a lotus leaf,
we are unable to shake it off. We are smeared
by it and our potential becomes shackled. The
mind is imprisoned by the past failure and
continuously doubts itself. Success can also
become a mental burden. While it is natural to
delight in success, such delight can become
obsessive. One may be so absorbed in a single
act of success, recalling it to others and expecting
continuous acclaim from them, that the
achievement of success becomes a prison in
which the mind lives and fails to achieve its

potential. To offer one's actions to God is to live, not in the failures and successes of the past, but in the present moment, the moment of opportunity and action.

Chapter 8

Finding Happiness in the Self

"As a lamp in a windless place does not flicker",
is the simile used for the yogi of controlled mind,
practicing concentration on the Self (6:19)[10]

In this striking simile, Krishna describes
the state of mind of one who knows the self and
whose attention is centered there. To give us a
glimpse of this mental state, he uses the image of

---

[10] *yathā dīpo nivātastho*
neṅgate sopamā smṛtā
yogino yatacittasya
yuñjato yogam ātmanaḥ

a flame in a windless location. It is not a location without air, but where there is minimal movement in the atmosphere. A flame is unsteady and easily affected by air currents surrounding it. Its movements reflect the changing direction and intensity of the wind to which it is exposed. When a flame is tossed around by the wind, the light which it emits varies in intensity. It is not evenly distributed, but dispersed and scattered. If the motion in the air subsides, the same flame becomes steady. It does not flicker, but burns with a silent intensity. Its light is evenly distributed and all objects within its range are illumined.

There are many good reasons for comparing the mind to a flame. Like a flame which emits light and helps us gain knowledge of the external world, the mind is an instrument of knowledge. With the aid of the five senses, we apprehend the world through the mind. Like a flame the mind is wavering and in motion. Arjuna (6:34) complained to Krishna about the fickle nature of the mind.

> The mind is indeed restless, Krishna. It is turbulent, strong and stubborn. It is as difficult to restrain as is the wind.

Krishna (6:35) concurs with Arjuna that the mind is unsteady and difficult to control. He recommends constant effort and detachment arising from an understanding of the limitations of desire.

If the restlessness of a flame is caused by the wind and if it could be calmed by placing it in a tranquil atmosphere, what causes mental restlessness and how may this be overcome? The restlessness of the mind, in Hinduism, is an expression of its search. The destination of this search is liberation (*mokṣa*), which is freedom from meaninglessness and the attainment of peace and fullness. In the quest for liberation, we develop desires of various kinds. These include the desires for wealth, power, and prestige. We seek these in the hope of finding some form of lasting security and well-being. We also seek pleasures of various kinds, especially those centered on the enjoyment of sense objects.

Desires, like these, leave us unfulfilled. All sense experiences, however pleasurable, are finite. They have a beginning and an end and leave us wanting. Gains such as fame and power are also limited. They keep us anxious and restless, since we can never have enough of these to be contented. We always feel threatened by the achievements of others.

If the fulfillment and security which we
seek cannot be found in material accumulation,
sense-pleasure, power or fame, where is it to be
found? From the Hindu standpoint, the problem
is in the search itself. The search is based on the
assumption that the self is inadequate and
incomplete and that gains of various kinds are
necessary for its adequacy. This presumption
about the self, teaches Hinduism, is erroneous.
The self (ātman) is not what we take it to be. We
look outside of ourselves, ignoring the truth
which is right before us. Our predicament is not
unlike that of the customs officer at the border
checkpoint. Each day, for years, a trader
crossed the border with several donkeys carrying
weighty sacks. The officer felt certain that the
man was smuggling something, but could not
discover anything illegal. On his final day of
work, he could not restrain his curiosity.
Assuring the man of immunity, he took him into
his office and begged him to reveal what he was
smuggling across the border all these years.
"Please tell me the truth," implored the customs
officer. "Donkeys," the trader calmly answered.

Unlike the body which is inert, the self is
of the nature of consciousness. If the eye sees,
the ear hears, the skin feels, the tongue tastes
and the mind thinks, it is because of the presence
of the self. The body is born, grows, changes and
dies, but the self is timeless and indestructible.

Happiness is the nature of the self and not the content of any object. The same object which appears to be the source of my joy today, becomes the cause of my unhappiness tomorrow. In addition, one object or person can, at the same time, be a cause for joy and sorrow in different persons. Why do we experience happiness in the attainment of a desired object? The existence of a desire in the mind induces a restlessness for its fulfillment. When the object is gained, the agitations disappear in the satisfied condition of one's mind. In this contented mind, the happiness, which is the nature of the self, is experienced. The gain of the object only serves to bring about the appropriate mental condition in which this ever-present happiness is known.

When one understands the self to be consciousness which is timeless bliss, one becomes satisfied in the self. One no longer searches for happiness, since it is known to be one's own nature. Having understood happiness to be the nature of the self, the mind does not wander restlessly in a vain search from object to object. It becomes an abiding and restful mind, like a bee finding its nectar in a flower. When the agitations of desire subside, the mind, like a flame in a windless room, rests calmly in the self. There is peace in the midst of all activities.

Chapter 9

The Unity of Life

Nothing higher than Me exists, Arjuna.
Everything that exists is strung on me like jewels
on a string (7:7)[11]

We may begin our discussion on this simile
by reflecting on the ways in which God is
superior to all that exists. God may be said to
be higher than all things because of God's
transcendence of time. God existed before all
things, and brings all things into existence. The
entire creation depends on God for its
origination and sustenance. While God is the
cause of the creation, God is uncaused and

---

[11]*mattaḥ parataram nānyat*
kiṁcid asti dhanaṁjaya
mayi sarvam idaṁ protaṁ
sūtre maṇigaṇā iva

independent. God is not only the source of the
creation, but also the place of its dissolution.
When the world order comes to an end, God will
be.

Second, God may be described to be
higher than everything in the sense that God is
greater and larger than all things. The universe
is larger than we thought it was. It stretches
beyond the reach of our most sophisticated
telescopes. This universe of incomparable
vastness exists, however, in space. Space and the
universe exist in God. God is described in the
Upanishads as larger than the largest and smaller
than the smallest. God is greater than anything
we can imagine, since whatever we can imagine
is contained in God.

Consider the implications of a recent
discovery. In 1987, an astronomer in Chile
witnessed the explosion of a supernova. It was a
powerful explosion which was estimated to have
released as much energy as our sun will produce
in 10 billion years. While the explosion was
witnessed in 1987, it did not occur in that year.
The supernova exploded 170,000 years before.
The light released by the explosion, took 170,000
years to reach earth, traveling at a speed of 6
trillion miles a year! The dimensions of the
universe which exist in God are astounding to
contemplate.

Third, God is higher than all things because God is the goal and end of all human search and longing. Human desires find their true fulfillment in God. We all desire a happiness which is lasting and a peace that endures. God is the happiness and peace which we long for, knowingly or unknowingly. There is no doubt that one experiences happiness and security through pleasures and gains of various kinds, but these are transient and uncertain in nature.

In this simile, one of the most beautiful in the text, Krishna helps us to understand the relationship between God and the world. He describes the universe as being strung on him like jewels on a string. This is a profoundly suggestive analogy, illuminating many facts of the Hindu understanding of the relationship between God and the world.

A jewel is a desirable object of value. It is attractive and cherished by the owner who takes delight in it. By comparing the created world with a jewel, Krishna is indicating his value for the creation and how precious all things are to him. The Upanishads describe God as deliberating over the creation and creating all things out of bliss. In this simile, we get a view of the creation as God sees it, and of the delight which God takes in the world. Like a

purposefully made necklace of jewels, no being
is redundant or without value in the eyes of God.

The simile also suggests that even as a row
of gems is supported and held together by its
string, the creation is held together and sustained
by God. A string gives order and symmetry to a
row of gems. Similarly, God gives harmony and
order to the creation. Without the string, there
may be individual jewels, but not a necklace.
Without God, the particular objects of the
creation do not constitute a cosmos or a
harmonious order.

The image of a string through a row of
jewels also informs us that God does not sustain
the world by being remote and distant from it,
but by being intimately present in everything.
The Hindu understanding of the relationship
between God and the world is not deistic. Deism
suggests that the relationship between God and
the universe is like that between a watchmaker
and a watch. A watchmaker manufactures a
watch, but the product exists and functions on its
own after it is made. It does not depend moment
to moment on its creator. The universe, on the
other hand, has no existence or reality apart
from God. If God is not, the universe is not.
Creation is not separate from God spatially or
temporally.

The string which runs through each jewel in a necklace supports the arrangement, but is also the common reality in each one. The gems are different in form, but the string is one and the same. The string links and unites each gem with the other, however separate they are spatially. In an analogous way, God is the common and unifying reality in all created things, however different each one may appear to be. God is the one truth in each one of us, uniting us with each other and with all things. Each gem is attractive on its own, but there is a special beauty when they are brought together in the arrangement of a necklace. The string makes this possible. Similarly, the beauty of human existence is poignantly expressed through relationships with each other which gain significance when we discern the same God in the heart of all.

Finally, in what is the ultimate paradox of the simile, the string which supports, sustains and unifies the arrangement of jewels is not usually seen. Our eyes focus on the jewels, while the string remains invisible. Yet the beauty and order of the necklace is evidence of the presence of the string. In the absence of the string, the arrangement falls apart. The beauty, order and purposefulness of the creation continue to disclose the reality of the creator. Yet, even as one can admire and become attached to a necklace while ignoring the string, one can become engrossed in the world and be forgetful of God, its creator and sustainer. The simile calls us to see both. To see the world and ignore God is as one-sided as seeing God and ignoring the world. The world does not exist independently of God who is present in all things. To see God in all things and all things in God is true seeing.

Chapter 10

All Exist in God

As the mighty wind blowing everywhere dwells
constantly in space, know that, in the same
manner, all beings exist in Me (9:6)[12]

The previous simile helped us to
understand better the relationship between God
and the world. Krishna compared himself to a
string supporting a necklace of jewels. God
supports the universe by being present in the
heart of everything. Every analogy, however,
has its limits. While the analogy of a necklace is
meant to draw our attention to the immanence of
God, one may come away with the impression

---

[12] *yathākāśasthito nityaṁ*
vāyuḥ sarvatrago mahān
tathā sarvāṇi bhūtāni
matsthānīty upadhāraya

that God exists only within the universe and that God is limited to and bound to the world. The analogy before us, of wind and space, corrects this erroneous conclusion.

As human beings, we are endowed with many abilities. Among these are the ability to know, to desire and to create. There are limits to all of our abilities. Our bodies, for example, are mortal and limited by space. At any particular time, we can be present physically only at one place. While we have the power of acquiring and increasing our knowledge, we are not omniscient. The more we know, the more we realize how much we do not know.

With bodies limited by time and space and minds circumscribed in knowledge, our powers of creation are also finite. When we wish to create something, we must use material already available in the creation. We cannot create out of nothing. We are also separate spatially from the things which we create, since these do not exist within us. An artist may fashion a sculpture from an image within her mind, but the artist and the work of art exist in space and are separate from each other. Time also separates us from the things which we create. We cannot cling forever to the things which we create, since our mortality will ensure physical separation.

As beings in space and time, our imaginations also operate within these limits even when we think of God. We think of God as greater and grander than us, but still imagine God within the limits of space and time. Even when we think of God as creator, we still imagine God to create in ways which are similar to us. We begin with space and locate God somewhere in space, usually above us. This seems to accord with our belief that God, as our creator, must be spatially higher than us. God's world is imagined to be similar to ours, but grander and more beautiful. From there, God creates our universe outside of Godself and is separate from it, just as we are separate from the things which we create.

The problem with such images is that they limit God by visualizing God as a being in space. They are contradictory because they usually posit God as existing at some particular space, while, at the same time, claiming God to be everywhere. From the Hindu standpoint, we cannot assume space and time to be eternal, since they are created realities. Before creation, God alone exists. There is no space or time. Space is the first of the five created elements, the others being air, heat, water, and minerals. Since God alone exists before creation, space and the entire created order exist within the divine. It is true that God is in all things, but this claim has to be complemented by the understanding that all things are in God. God is greater than the universe and not limited by any created object. All beings and things exist in God, just as the mighty wind, moving everywhere, exists in space.

Space accommodates the entire universe. We cannot conceive a universe without space. Yet, there is a transcendent quality about space. It retains its nature and is not altered or changed by any event transpiring within it. It does not move, while permitting movement of all kinds within it. It supports all things, while not getting entangled with anything. In a similar way, the universe exists in God, without limiting or bringing about any change in the nature of God. In relation to the universe, God is both immanent and transcendent.

This simile is a powerful reminder that we can never be separate from God. Nothing can live outside of God. Our separation from God is primarily a separation of ignorance, since God is eternally here and now.

The image of a mighty wind raging in the stillness of space is very instructive. God is the stillness and peace which we long for. Yet, this peace is not to be thought of as existing outside of us. It is not a separate object to be gained and possessed. This center of calm is not outside of the world to be reached and attained after death. We live in it here and now. It is at the core of our beings awaiting our discovery. If we discover it, we may not be able to avoid the storms of life, but we can navigate these from a point of stillness and peace and not be blown around helplessly on the ocean of life.

Chapter 11

The Purity of the Self

As the all-pervasive space, because of its
subtlety, is not polluted, so the self, present
everywhere in the body, is not polluted (13:32)[13]

In thinking about God, as the last simile
reminded us, we must not imagine God to be an
object in space. The truth is that space and
everything within space exist in God. All things
are in God, just as God is in all things. In the
simile before us, Krishna uses the analogy of
space once again. On this occasion, his purpose is

---

[13] *yathā sarvagataṁ saukṣmyād*
ākāśaṁ nopalipyate
sarvatrāvasthito dehe
tathātmā nopalipyate

to explain how the self (*ātman*), can be associated with the body while, at the same time, be free from the qualities and characteristics of the body.

The human physical body comes into being at the time of conception, grows, changes, ages and dies. The self is the indweller in the body, the one for whom the body is an instrument. It is the seer in the eyes, the hearer in the ear, the taster in the tongue, the smeller in the nose and the feeler in the skin. Existing in every organ and cell of the body, the self makes life possible.

While the body is subject to birth and death, the self, as we have already learnt, is immortal. It does not come into being with the body or cease to be when the body dies. How is it possible for the self which is seated everywhere in the body to remain untouched by the nature of the body? To help us understand this, Krishna uses the analogy of space.

Space is everywhere the same and all things exist in space. Space cannot be divided or severed into parts by any means. Fire, which burns objects in space, cannot burn space itself. Rain and thunderstorms may soak and flood the earth, but are unable to moisten space. The wind which blows around in space cannot move space. Space accommodates all the elements, but is not affected by their activities. How does space manage to retain its nature? The reason, explains Krishna, is the subtlety of space.

In the Hindu understanding, the universe is composed of five great elements: space, air, heat, water, and minerals. The subtlety of an element is measured by its pervasiveness. Space is regarded as the subtlest of all the elements because it is all-pervasive. Air is considered to be subtler than water and water is subtler than any mineral. Subtlety is also measured by the tangibility or intangibility of a particular element. The subtler an element, the less available it is for experience through the senses. Minerals, for example, can be seen, heard, tasted, touched and smelt. Water can be seen, heard, felt, and tasted. Water has no distinctive smell. Fire, as heat, can be seen, heard and felt, but not tasted or smelt. Air can be heard and felt, but not seen, tasted, or smelt. Space is understood, in Hindu cosmology, to possess only the quality of sound and viewed, therefore, as the subtlest of the five elements.

Subtler than space is the self. It is truly all-pervasive since space itself exists in the self. The self cannot be known by any of the five senses. It cannot be seen, heard, touched, tasted or smelt. If space is not polluted by any element existing within it, the self, which is subtler than space, is always pure. The presence of the body within the self does not alter its nature.

The same is true of the relationship between the self and the mind. The self is present in every thought and modification of the mind. Without the self as consciousness, there is no possibility of thoughts of any kind. These, however, do not cause any change in the nature of the self. In relation to thoughts, the self is like a lamp. A lamp in a room provides the illumination which enables us to perform various actions. We may sit in the room and devise plans to help the needy or we may plot a scheme to defraud someone. The light is present for both types of actions, but not affected by the choices made in the room. In a similar manner, the self as awareness illumines all thoughts in the mind. It reveals good as well as evil thoughts. This does not mean that there are no differences between good and evil thoughts. Good thoughts are preferable since a virtuous mind alone can know the self. The point is that mental states, like physical characteristics, do not change the self.

The self is what we are and we must understand the body to be an instrument. An instrument, like a pair of glasses, ought to be properly cared for, but must not be regarded as oneself. The self does not have to be separated physically from the body to be liberated. As the simile reminds us, it is always free and pure. Liberation does not have to await the death of the body, since the problem is not the existence of the body, but taking the body to be identical with the self. The same is true for the mind. While the self shines in every thought, it is not transformed by any mental state or condition. It is always itself.

Chapter 12

The Self As Awareness

Just as one sun illumines this entire world,
so the lord of the field illumines
the entire field (13:33)[14]

In the last simile which we discussed,
Krishna used the example of space to illustrate
the purity of the self in relation to the body and
mind. Although the self exists throughout the
body, it is not affected by the characteristics of
the body, even as space is not altered by any
object or event occurring within it. Space is the
subtlest of all elements, but subtler than space is
the self.

---

[14] *yathā prakāśayaty ekaḥ*
kṛtsnaṁ lokam imaṁ raviḥ
kṣetraṁ kṣetrī tathā kṛtsnaṁ
prakāśayati bhārata

The simile before us explains the nature of
the self as the illuminator of the body and mind
complex. To help us understand this aspect of the
nature of the self, Krishna turns to one of the
most familiar objects in our daily experience, the
sun.

The sun reveals the objects in our world. It
is when an object is bathed in the light of the
sun's rays that we are able to perceive it with our
eyes. In the absence of the light of the sun,
nothing is seen. Everything will be enveloped in
an obscuring darkness. Light is the very nature of
the sun. If the sun ceased to be a source of light,
it would cease to be. We cannot think of the sun
but as the illuminator of our world.

The objects of the world are countless in
number and possess different characteristics. The
sun which reveals and illumines these objects is
one. The objects illuminated are many, but the
illuminator is one. The one sun illumines all
objects impartially. It does not bestow its light on
some objects and withhold it from others. Large
and small, pure and impure, beautiful and ugly,
all receive the light of the sun equally.

The sun is the source of heat which makes
life itself possible. In the absence of the light of
the sun, our planet will quickly become cold and

lifeless. Other conditions of life might be present, but the vital ingredient would be missing.

Just as the one sun illumines our entire world, says Krishna, the lord of the field illumines the field. At the beginning of chapter thirteen, Krishna introduces the terminology of the field and the knower of the field. The field corresponds to the body and mind and the knower of the field is the self.

The body is referred to as a field, because it is the location of activities of various kinds. The seeds of *karma* sowed through actions in the past bear fruit in the body. Like a field, the body is known. Even as the sun illumines and makes known the objects in the world, the body is known to us. It can be experienced through all the senses. As an object of knowledge, the body is the field. It is not the self.

Is the self identical with the senses? With my eyes, I can see my body, but are my eyes known or unknown? My eyes are obviously known since I am aware of them and aware of any defect in them. The self (the knower) is not the organ of sight or any other sense organ.

Is the self the mind? The senses, after all, depend on the mind for their efficient functioning. Even a healthy eye does not see anything within its range if the mind is distracted or inattentive. The same is true for the other senses. If my mind is sad, angry, restless or bored, I consider myself to be identical with these states. Are these mental conditions known or unknown? Is the restless mind an object of awareness? Since one is aware of it, the mind is known and cannot be the knower. Thoughts and emotions come and go, but the knower is there before, during and after any particular thought.

The self is not the body, mind or the senses since it is aware of all three. Like the sun which illumines all objects, the self reveals the body, senses and the mind. It makes the existence of these known. The nature of the self is awareness.

The common characteristic in the sun and the self is the ability to reveal and make things known. Objects in the world are many and the sun which illumines them is one. The self reveals the body and mind, but is the self, unlike the sun, different in each body? Is this where the analogy varies? My body, senses and mind are obviously different from yours and, if the self is identified with any one or all of these, the self cannot be one. The self, as we have discussed above, is awareness. Our bodies differ, but I am aware of my body and you are aware of yours. The same is true for our senses and minds. The awareness, because of which we both know our minds and bodies, does not differ. Like the sun, the self is one and the same in all beings. Bodies and minds, like the objects in the world, are different, but the self, like the sun, is one.

The self illumines all bodies and minds. It is present in every mind, whatever its intellectual or moral disposition. Goodness of heart and mind is necessary for self-knowledge, but the reality of the self is not limited by mental states.

While the luminosity and oneness of the sun make it a good analogy for helping us to understand the nature of the self, there are important differences. The sun illumines all objects, but the sun does not illumine the self. The self is not revealed by anything. It is self-revealed. Everyone knows that he or she exists and the indubitable sense of one's existence arises from the reality of the self. Everything is revealed by the self which is awareness. In the effulgence of awareness, even the light of the sun is known. It is the light of all lights.

Knowing the self as awareness in all beings helps us to understand its identity in all. One learns to see oneself in all and to regard the joys and sorrows of others as one's own. This is the meaning of compassion.

Suggested Reading

Swami Chinmayananda, *The Holy Geeta* (Bombay: Central Chinmaya Mission Trust, 1995)

Swami Dayananda, *The Teaching of the Bhagavadgita* (Rishikesh: Sri Gangadhareswar Trust, 1985).

S. Radhakrishnan, *The Bhagavadgita* (London: Allen and Unwin, 1976).

Anantanand Rambachan, *Gītāmṛtam: The Essential Teachings of the Bhagavadgita* (Delhi: Motilal Banarsidass, 1996).

Alladi Mahadeva Sastry, *The Bhagavadgita with the commentary of Sri Sankaracharya* (Madras: Samata Books, 1979).

Srimad Bhagavadgita (Gorakhpur: Gita Press, 1973).